10 Sharks Bigger Than Great White Sharks

10 Sharks Bigger Than Great White Sharks

Sydney Austin

Published in 2022 by THP Kidz ZOne
An imprint of Tamarind Hill Press Limited
14023099

ISBN: 978-1-915161-16-1

For bulk orders, contact business@tamarindhillpress.com

Copyright © Sydney Austin 2022

Sydney Austin asserts her right to be identified as the author of this work in accordance with the Copyright, Design and Patents Act of 1988.

All rights reserved. No part of this publication, may be reproduced, stored in a retrievable system, or transmitted in any form or by any means, electronic, mechanical photocopying, recording or otherwise, without the permission of the author and copyright owner.

Table of Contents

Introduction 6
Facts About the Greenland Shark 8
Facts About the Great Hammerhead Shark 11
Facts About the Megamouth Shark 14
Facts About the Pacific Sleeper Shark 17
Facts About the Thresher Shark 20
Facts About the Ginsu Shark 23
Facts About the Otodus Shark 26
Facts About the Basking Shark 29
Facts About the Whale Shark 32
Facts About the Megalodon Shark 35
Conclusion 37
About the Author 38

Introduction

One of Earth's most fascinating creatures is the shark. These apex predators are a very diversified group of animals that have ruled our waters for ages, with over 500 species swimming in the water.

From the great hammerhead shark, which is the largest of all hammerhead sharks, to the enormous whale shark, there are many different types and sizes of sharks. Continue reading to find out more about these amazing animals as we list the 10 sharks that are larger than the great white.

Greenland Shark

Facts About the Greenland Shark

The Greenland shark, often referred to as the grey, ground, gurry, or sleeping shark (for its lethargic behaviour) is the world's oldest vertebrate and can live to be 400 years old or more. The scientific name for the Greenland shark is Somniosus (meaning sleep) microcephalus (meaning little head), which loosely translates to "sleepy little-head." The tissue at the centre of its lens, which keeps expanding throughout the course of its lifetime, is radiocarbon-dated to determine how old it is.

Greenland sharks can grow up to a maximum length of 21 feet and weigh up to 900 kg, despite having small heads. They feature tiny eyes, small, sharp teeth, and short, rounded snouts. In proportion to the size of their bodies, their gill slits and dorsal and pectoral fins are similarly relatively little. On their dorsal (top) sides or down their flanks, some of them may have dark lines or white patches in addition to their brown, grey, or black colouring.

The Greenland shark is related to southern and Pacific sleeper shark. And just like the sleeper shark, the Greenland shark lives in very deep, cold parts of the ocean. Greenland sharks, which are unique to the northern Atlantic Ocean, are built to survive in extremely cold, deep waters.

Though they are enormous, they pose no threat to people and are one of the slowest sharks that exist.

The Greenland shark eats just about anything. These include but are not limited to bottom-dwelling and oceanic fish, as well as other sharks, skates, eels, seals, amphipods, small cetaceans, seabirds, marine snails, jellyfish, squids, brittle stars, crabs, and sea urchins.

Great Hammerhead Shark

Facts About the Great Hammerhead Shark

There are nine different hammerhead species, and several of them face extinction. Great hammerhead sharks are one such endangered species. They are natural predators and can move over great distances, up to 756 miles (1,200 km). These sharks can grow larger than great white sharks and are also one of the oddest species of sharks in existence.

Great hammerheads can reach lengths of 20 feet. They have flat, hammer-shaped heads with an edge-to-edge notch in the middle. Cephalofoils, the name for their unusually shaped heads, offer them 360-degree fields of vision. The front edge of a young hammerhead is slightly bent, becoming virtually straight as it grows older. The roughly rectangular skull of this species makes it easily identifiable. The second dorsal and pelvic fins are high with profoundly concave posterior margins, whereas the first dorsal fin is very high and curved. Electrical detectors in their brains allow them to detect possible prey, especially those buried in the sand.

Great hammerheads are semi-oceanic and can exclusively be found in warm, shallow coastal seas that are at least 68 degrees, on island terraces, continental shelf, passages, and lagoons. They can be found in the world's waters at depths between one and three hundred meters.

Great hammerhead sharks, like other hammerhead species, use their hammer-shaped heads to locate and consume prey. They typically eat stingrays, cephalopods (octopus and squid), crabs, other sharks that graze on the ocean floor, and bony fish. Great hammerheads have been photographed pinning down their preferred prey, stingrays, on the sides of their heads while consuming the ray's wings. They only pursue stingray-sized prey. Because of how large great hammerhead sharks are, they are not prey to other marine animals.

Megamouth Shark

Facts About the Megamouth Shark

One of the most peculiar-looking sharks in the water is the megamouth shark. Its scientific name is Megachasma pelagios. The megamouth's enormous, round mouth is its most distinguishing characteristic and is what gives it its name. The mouth is roughly four feet. These sharks have a noticeable long, spherical snout and a huge terminal mouth. Megamouth sharks have a jaw that extends past the eyes.

Megamouth sharks have a white ventral side and a grey dorsal side. Dark markings can be seen under the lower jaws of megamouth sharks. Small-hooked teeth are scattered around the top and bottom jaws. Megamouth sharks have a short pelvic fin, a small, pointed anal fin, and two pointed dorsal fins. They also have two pectoral fins that taper. The megamouth shark can weigh up to 2700 pounds (1215 kg) and grow up to 18 feet long.

Although megamouth sharks are among the largest sharks in our oceans, they are rarely seen. They are not dangerous to people. Megamouth sharks can be found in the Pacific, Atlantic, and Indian Oceans and tend to swim in warm, tropical environments. They spend the day on the ocean floor and only approach the surface at night to feed. They have only ever been observed a few times in the wild. Reports of sightings have been in places like Australia, Africa, Mexico, and the Philippines.

Megamouth sharks, similar to basking sharks and whale sharks, are filter feeders, swimming with their mouths open wide to catch their prey which are solely plankton, the smallest organism in the water.

Pacific Sleeper Shark

Facts About the Pacific Sleeper Shark

The Pacific sleeper shark is known by the scientific name somniosus pacificus. These sharks stand out from more common sharks like tiger sharks or bull sharks with their small, flattened dorsal fins that are blue-black in colour.

They are deep-water sharks. The body is cylindrical, the two dorsal fins are equal in size, and the snout is small and rounded. The pectoral fins are farther from the pelvic fins than the first dorsal one. Additionally, there are a few tiny precaudal fins, and the caudal fin (tail) has an asymmetrical shape and a prominent ventral (lower) lobe. It is believed that the largest Pacific sleeper sharks, which are larger than great white sharks, can reach lengths of up to 23 feet (males can grow up to 4.4 meters in length and 4.3 for females). Still, the largest confirmed Pacific sleeper shark was larger than all great white sharks save for the greatest, weighing in at 1,958 pounds which is almost a ton.

The Pacific sleeper shark has two different types of teeth, unlike the majority of shark species. Their bottom teeth are flattened and jagged, while their upper teeth are pointed and thin. As opportunistic feeders, they consume practically anything that comes in their way, even carrion.

The Pacific sleeper shark inhabits the temperate seas of the North Pacific between the latitudes of 70°N and 47°S, from Japan to the Bering Sea along with southern California in the United States, Baja California, and Mexico. Some sightings have reportedly been reported in the South Pacific. The Pacific sleeper shark can be found in Australian waters from seamounts south of Tasmania to the Challenger Plateau off eastern New Zealand, and perhaps even as far north as Macquarie Island. Off the coast of Uruguay, they can be observed in the southwest Atlantic.

In addition to bottom fish, octopuses, squids, including giant squids and its much larger relative, colossal squids, crabs, and tritons, Pacific sleeper sharks also occasionally eat harbour seals, Steller sea lions, and carrion.

Thresher Shark

Facts About the Thresher Shark

Thresher sharks, Alopias vulpinus, are also known as Atlantic threshers, big-eye threshers, common threshers, fox sharks, grayfishes, green threshers, sea foxes, slashers, swingletails, swiveltails, thintail threshers, thrashers, and thresher shark. They are now classified as Vulnerable and have never been connected to a human attack. They are, regrettably, frequently hunted by fishermen for their fins, which are used to make shark fin soup.

They are some of the biggest predatory sharks in the ocean and are distinguished by their extraordinarily long tails. Greater thresher sharks bigger than the great white are pretty common. The teeth of these sharks are tiny, curved, smooth, and extremely sharp. Both their upper and lower jaws' teeth have comparable shapes. Thresher sharks have dorsal (upper) and ventral (under) sides that range in colour from white to metallic brown to blue. These sharks can reach lengths of 24 feet (maximum length of 7.6 m for males and 5.5 m for females), with their unique tail accounting for up to half of that length.

Thresher sharks can be found in warm, temperate waters. Although they tend to favour cool oceanic waters, they will occasionally stray into coastal areas in search of fish. Young threshers are frequently spotted in shallow waters and near to shore.

Threshers swim into schools of fish and thrash their long, scythe-like tail to stun the fish, before catching them to eat. Thresher sharks consume small pelagic fish, such as squid, hake, mackerel, anchovies, and sardines.

Ginsu Shark

Facts About the Ginsu Shark

The Ginsu shark was one of the largest sharks of its day, named after the renowned sharp Ginsu knife and are scientifically referred to as Cretoxyrhina mantelli. Ginsu sharks were common in the 107–73 million-year-old oceans. They, therefore, serve as a predecessor to the enormous Megalodon.

It shared similarities with the present great white shark in terms of look and build. The three-inch-long teeth of the Ginsu shark can be used to assess its size. Great white teeth are only two inches long as a reference. The Ginsu shark had recurved, 2-inch (5-centimetre) teeth that resemble knives. These teeth were much wider and more robust than those of a mako, and each possessed a smooth-edged blade with an extraordinarily thick enamelled coating designed for slicing and stabbing its prey. They may have grown to about 30 feet in length.

The Ginsu shark appears to have favoured shallow subtropical oceans to tropical ones for its habitat, which is uncommon for the majority of mackerel sharks today.

The adult Ginsu shark appears to have mostly eaten marine reptiles, such as mosasaurs and plesiosaurs, along with big, bony fish on occasion.

Otodus Shark

Facts About the Otodus Shark

The word "otodus" means ear-shaped tooth. Otodus was a mackerel shark, like the megalodon and modern great white sharks. Despite being small, mackerel sharks also include salmon and porbeagle sharks. This shark would make the largest great white sharks look like a dwarf if it were alive today.

According to estimates, the sharks in the genus otodus could have reached a length of 40 feet or more.

In comparison to great white teeth, which are about two inches long, their teeth are around five inches long and triangular-shaped with smooth cutting edges, noticeable cusps on the roots, and a triangular crown. Additionally, some otodus teeth exhibit evidence of developing serrations.

Large bony fish and possibly even other sharks were the staple diet of these macro predators.

The otodus shark could be found in oceans worldwide.

Basking Shark

Facts About the Basking Shark

The second-largest existing shark in the world, basking shark (Cetorhinus maximus), has one of the most peculiar appearances of any shark. They have conical snouts, sub-terminal mouths, extraordinarily wide gill slits, dark bristle-like gill rakers (present throughout the year), powerful caudal keels, and big lunate (curved) tails. They have many tiny teeth. Their bodies range in hue from grey/brown to slate-grey to black, with lighter spots occasionally seen on the dorsal side. The ventral side is paler and frequently has white patches along the ventral side or under the snout and lips. Only the whale shark is bigger than it in terms of size.

Basking sharks can reach lengths of over 26 feet, or the width of a school bus. Though they consume plankton, which are the tiniest aquatic organisms, these sharks are anything but maneaters. They are currently classified as Endangered, with pollution and overfishing as their main threats.

Basking sharks can be found worldwide in Arctic and temperate waters. Nearly every shoreline bordering the Atlantic and Pacific Oceans has seen them; people typically observe them at or near the surface. They often appear in the winter and spring along the west coast of North America, from British Columbia to Baja California. In regions of the North Atlantic, this pattern is reversed.

Whale Shark

Facts About the Whale Shark

One of the most recognizable sharks on the earth is the whale shark (Rhincodon typus). They are also listed as Endangered due to overfishing and pollution. Whale sharks are the largest living sharks in the world. Though they are huge, they are gentle and can grow to heights of more than 60 feet, making them roughly three times larger than even the biggest great white sharks.

At the front of their heads, they have an incredibly large mouth that is unusual (rather than on the underside like most sharks). They feature two dorsal fins and two pectoral fins, as well as wide, flat skulls, rounded snouts, small eyes, and five very big gill slits. Just behind the shark's eye lies the spiracle, a relict first gill slit for breathing while the animal is submerged. The upper fin of its tail is a little larger than the lower fin.

Although a 60-foot shark may appear to be a frightening creature, they are in no way a threat to people. Whale shark ecotourism is becoming more and more well-liked. All around the world, these sharks can be found in tropical environments where they eat plankton. Whale sharks are filter feeders, just like baleen whales. Whale sharks have incredibly thick, dark grey skin that can be up to 10 cm thick. They are speckled with characteristic light-yellow or white markings (random stripes and dots). On each side of their bodies, three pronounced ridges may be seen.

With the exception of the Mediterranean, whale sharks are found throughout all tropical and mild temperate oceans. They prefer water temperatures about 21–30°C while feeding on the surface during the day. However, at night and when moving, they frequently descend to depths of more than 700m.

Megalodon Shark

Facts About the Megalodon Shark

The word "megalodon," means "large tooth." Researchers have never directly seen the megalodon, therefore they can only hypothesize about its general look. Many of them believe it resembled a big white shark in appearance. The megalodon lived from 23 million years ago to about 2.6 million years ago.

The megalodon is said to be the largest shark that nature has ever seen. These sharks, which were larger than great white sharks and could have easily eaten the largest sharks alive today, reached as long as 60 feet.

The astonishingly massive teeth that this species left behind are its most famous artefacts. Their teeth are bigger than the size of an adult human hand. These teeth supplied a large body with food while filling a huge pair of jaws.

The particular habitats megalodons frequented are not known for sure, but with the discovery of their teeth by researchers, the most common locations for this species of shark are temperate and tropical waters. Scientists can speculate about the depths these sharks lived in.

Adults just could not have survived in shallow coastal habitats due to their enormous size. Instead, they made their home in the open ocean, offshore.

Because no living tissue or fossilized stomach remains have been discovered, scientists are left to make only educated guesses regarding the nutrition of these species. The megalodon teeth were discovered close to the whale bones that had been bit. According to researchers, the shark's prey had to have been substantial enough to support such a massive body size. Given this, they may have consumed enormous marine creatures like whales. They could have consumed big fish and other sharks as well.

Conclusion

Sharks are special and distinctive from one another in numerous ways. From their individual characteristics to behavioral tendencies. And there is no doubt that some sharks are truly behemoths of the ocean when comparing the size of great white sharks to others. I hope that this book provided an interesting look at the biggest sharks of the oceanic world from those that formerly lived millions of years ago in addition to the largest sharks that are alive today.

About the Author

Having been a loner for most of her life, Sydney Austin took solace in reading. She sought out books to expand her knowledge and loved learning new things. Sydney describes herself as a being a big kid who is discovering different things as they grow. Her love for kids combined with her love for science gave birth to *10 Sharks Bigger Than Great White Sharks*.